I0408948

Unlock the Power of Your Mind and Money: Your Guide to Financial and Mental Well-Being

ISBN: 9798862309881

Financial Disclaimer

The information provided in this book, "Unlock the Power of Your Mind and Money: Your Guide to Financial and Mental Well-Being," is intended for educational and informational purposes only. The author, publisher, and contributors are not financial advisors, and the content in this book should not be construed as professional financial, investment, or legal advice.

The content in this book is based on the author's knowledge and research as of the publication date. The financial landscape is dynamic and subject to change, and new developments may have occurred since the last update.

Readers are strongly encouraged to consult with qualified financial advisors, legal professionals, or other experts before making any financial, investment, or legal decisions. The author and publisher do not make any guarantees, representations, or warranties regarding the accuracy, completeness, or suitability of the information provided in this book. Any reliance on the information in this book is at the reader's own risk.

The author and publisher disclaim any liability for any direct, indirect, incidental, special, or consequential damages arising from the use of or reliance on the information in this book, or any actions or decisions made based on the content herein. The reader acknowledges that there are no promises, guarantees, or assurances of specific financial outcomes or success by implementing the strategies or recommendations presented in this book.

Furthermore, the author and publisher disclaim any responsibility for the outcomes of financial, investment, or legal decisions made by readers. Readers are encouraged to conduct their own research, due diligence, and seek professional advice when necessary.

By reading this book, the reader agrees to release, indemnify, and hold harmless the author, publisher, and contributors from any and all claims, damages, liabilities, or expenses that may arise from the reader's use of or reliance on the information contained in this book.

This disclaimer serves as a legal notice that the content of this book is for informational purposes only, and the author and publisher are not responsible for any actions or decisions made by readers based on the content herein.

Chapter 1: The Psychology of Money

Money isn't just a tool for transactions; it's an emotional force that weaves its way through every facet of our lives. In this chapter, we'll delve into the intricate relationship between the human mind and money. Understanding the psychology of money is the first step toward achieving financial and mental well-being.

Understanding the Emotional Attachment to Money

Money is deeply rooted in our emotions and psychology. It's not merely a stack of bills or numbers in a bank account; it's a symbol of security, status, and even self-worth.

- **The Emotional Rollercoaster:** We often experience a range of emotions concerning money, from the elation of a windfall to the anxiety of mounting bills.

- **The Role of Childhood Experiences:** Our early experiences with money, witnessed through our parents or caregivers, can shape our financial behaviors and attitudes.

- **Money as a Measure of Success:** Society often equates financial success with personal success, leading us to tie our self-esteem to our financial standing.

- **Financial Anxiety and Guilt:** Financial stress, debt, or mismanagement can lead to persistent feelings of anxiety, guilt, and even depression.

Behavioral Economics and Money

Behavioral economics, a field that blends psychology and economics, has shed light on the way we make financial decisions.

- **Cognitive Biases:** Humans are susceptible to cognitive biases that can lead to irrational financial choices. For example, the availability bias makes us focus on recent financial events, potentially clouding our judgment.

- **Prospect Theory:** This theory explains how individuals often make choices based on perceived gains and losses, rather than objective facts. Loss aversion can lead us to take undue risks or avoid necessary financial decisions.

- **The Power of Framing:** How information is presented can drastically influence our financial choices. Understanding how marketers and advisors frame information can help you make more informed decisions.

Sources of Financial Stress

Financial stress is a common byproduct of the intricate relationship between money and psychology.

- **Statistics:** According to the American Psychological Association's 2021 Stress in America survey, money remains a significant source of stress for 64% of Americans.

- **Source:** APA's Stress in America Survey

- **Workplace Stress:** The demands of the workplace, job loss, or job uncertainty can take a toll on our mental well-being.

- **Debt and Financial Obligations:** Juggling multiple debts, bills, and financial obligations can lead to constant worry and anxiety.

- **Financial Goals vs. Reality:** Frustration often arises when financial goals seem unattainable due to unexpected expenses or slow progress.

Checklist: Assessing Your Emotional Relationship with Money

To begin your journey towards a healthier mind-money connection, take a moment to reflect:

- Do you associate your self-worth with your financial standing?
- How do you typically react to financial stress? Anxiety, avoidance, or impulsiveness?
- Can you identify any cognitive biases that have influenced your financial decisions in the past?

In the chapters to come, we'll explore strategies to navigate the emotional complexities of money, helping you build a more secure and balanced financial future while nurturing your mental health. Remember, understanding the psychology of money is the first step on this transformative journey.

Chapter 2: Mental Health and Financial Well-being

In this chapter, we'll delve into the profound connection between mental health and financial well-being. As you'll discover, these two aspects of your life are intricately interwoven, each influencing the other in profound ways. Understanding this link is essential for building a foundation of both financial and mental stability.

The Bi-directional Relationship: Mental Health Affects Finances and Vice Versa

It's crucial to recognize that mental health and financial well-being share a bi-directional relationship. One can impact the other, and this dynamic can significantly influence your life.

- **Mental Health Affects Finances:**

    o *Impaired Decision-Making:* Mental health struggles, such as depression or anxiety, can impair decision-making abilities, leading to financial choices that may not align with your best interests.

    o *Reduced Income and Employment Stability:* Severe mental health conditions can result in absenteeism, decreased work productivity, and even job loss, which can directly impact your financial stability.

    o *Increased Healthcare Costs:* Managing mental health conditions often entails medical expenses, including therapy, medication, and hospitalization, which can strain your budget.

- **Finances Affect Mental Health:**

    o *Stress and Anxiety:* Financial worries, debt, and financial instability can lead to persistent stress and anxiety, impacting your mental health.

    o *Depression and Self-esteem:* Struggles with debt, job loss, or financial setbacks can contribute to depression and negatively affect self-esteem.

    o *Relationship Strain:* Financial difficulties can lead to conflicts in relationships, contributing to emotional distress.

Common Mental Health Disorders and Their Financial Implications

Various mental health disorders can have significant financial implications, underscoring the importance of addressing mental health in conjunction with financial well-being.

- **Depression:**

    o *Statistics:* According to the World Health Organization (WHO), depression is a leading cause of disability worldwide, impacting over 264 million people.

    o *Financial Impact:* Individuals with depression may struggle with work absenteeism, reduced earning potential, and increased healthcare costs.

- **Anxiety Disorders:**

  o *Statistics:* Anxiety disorders affect over 40 million adults in the United States alone, according to the Anxiety and Depression Association of America (ADAA).

  o *Financial Impact:* Anxiety can lead to impulse spending, avoidance of financial responsibilities, and increased medical expenses due to stress-related health issues.

- **Bipolar Disorder:**

  o *Statistics:* Bipolar disorder affects approximately 2.8% of U.S. adults, reports the National Institute of Mental Health (NIMH).

  o *Financial Impact:* Individuals with bipolar disorder may experience manic episodes leading to reckless spending and depressive episodes that hinder financial planning.

The Stigma Surrounding Mental Health

Despite the prevalence of mental health conditions, a stigma persists, hindering open discussions and access to care.

- **Statistics:** According to the National Alliance on Mental Illness (NAMI), stigma remains one of the primary reasons people delay seeking mental health treatment.

- **Debunking Stigma:** It's crucial to challenge and debunk the stigma surrounding mental health by promoting open conversations, empathy, and support for those facing mental health challenges.

In the chapters that follow, we'll explore strategies to nurture both your mental health and financial well-being. By recognizing the bidirectional relationship between these two facets of your life, you can take proactive steps towards a balanced and prosperous future. Remember, mental health matters, and it's an integral part of your financial journey.

Chapter 3: The Vicious Cycle: Mental Health and Debt

Debt is not just a financial burden; it can also take a significant toll on your mental health. In this chapter, we'll explore the intricate relationship between mental health and debt, understanding how one can feed into the other in a seemingly never-ending cycle. Recognizing this connection is the first step towards breaking free and achieving financial and mental well-being.

The Connection Between Debt and Mental Health

Debt and mental health are often intertwined, with each affecting the other in various ways.

- **Financial Stress and Anxiety:** The burden of debt can lead to persistent stress and anxiety. The weight of financial obligations and the fear of not being able to meet them can keep you awake at night and dominate your thoughts during the day.

- **Depression and Hopelessness:** High levels of debt can contribute to feelings of depression and hopelessness. It may seem like an insurmountable mountain, with no end in sight.

- **Impact on Relationships:** Debt-related stress can strain relationships with family, friends, and partners. Arguments about money are a leading cause of relationship breakdowns.

Debt Management Strategies and Their Psychological Impact

Managing debt is not just about numbers; it's also about the psychological impact of the strategies you employ.

- **Debt Consolidation:** Combining multiple debts into one can make payments more manageable, reducing stress. However, it's essential to avoid accruing more debt after consolidation.

- **Debt Snowball vs. Debt Avalanche:** The psychological impact of choosing between these two strategies can be significant. The debt snowball focuses on paying off smaller debts first, providing a sense of accomplishment. The debt avalanche targets higher interest rate debts, saving money in the long run but requiring patience.

- **Credit Counseling:** Seeking the help of a credit counselor can alleviate stress by providing expert guidance and a structured repayment plan.

Case Studies of Individuals Breaking Free from the Debt-Mental Health Cycle

Real-life examples demonstrate that it's possible to break free from the debt-mental health cycle.

- **Case Study 1: Sarah's Debt-Free Journey:** Sarah accumulated significant credit card debt during a period of unemployment, leading to severe anxiety and depression. Through a combination of budgeting, debt consolidation, and therapy, she successfully paid off her debt and improved her mental health.

- **Case Study 2: Mark's Student Loan Struggles:** Mark faced overwhelming student loan debt, which affected his mental health and delayed important life milestones. He sought assistance from a financial counselor, adopted a strict budget, and engaged in stress-reduction techniques to regain control of his life.

Checklist: Assessing Your Debt and Mental Health

Before moving forward, assess your current situation:

- How does your debt make you feel? Anxious, stressed, depressed?
- Have you sought help or counseling for your debt-related stress?
- Are you aware of the specific debts that cause you the most anxiety?

In the chapters ahead, we'll explore strategies for managing debt while nurturing your mental health. Remember that breaking free from the debt-mental health cycle is a journey, but it's a journey worth taking for your well-being and financial stability.

Chapter 4: Stress and Decision-Making

Stress is a common companion on our financial journeys, but it can wreak havoc on our decision-making abilities. In this chapter, we'll explore the intricate relationship between stress and financial choices. By understanding how stress influences your decisions, you can take proactive steps to manage it and make more informed financial choices.

How Stress Affects Decision-Making

Stress, whether it's related to financial concerns or other life challenges, can significantly impact the way we make decisions.

- **The Fight-or-Flight Response:** Stress triggers our innate fight-or-flight response, which can lead to impulsive and sometimes irrational decisions. For instance, in a financial crisis, you might hastily liquidate investments or take on high-interest debt without considering the long-term consequences.

- **Cognitive Biases Amplified:** Stress can amplify cognitive biases like loss aversion and the endowment effect, making us more fearful of losing money and less willing to take calculated risks.

- **Short-Term Focus:** Stress often narrows our focus on immediate relief rather than long-term goals. This can result in neglecting crucial financial planning for the future.

Statistics: The Impact of Stress on Financial Decision-Making

Research indicates that stress can significantly affect financial decision-making.

- **Source:** A study published in the Journal of Behavioral Decision Making found that stress reduces individuals' willingness to take risks in financial decision-making, potentially leading to missed opportunities for growth.

- **Source:** The American Psychological Association's Stress in America survey highlights that stress negatively affects financial behaviors, such as spending and saving.

Strategies for Managing Stress in Financial Decision-Making

Managing stress is crucial for making sound financial choices. Here are steps to help you cope with stress effectively:

- **Step 1: Recognize Stress Triggers:**

    o Identify situations or factors that trigger stress related to your finances. Is it unexpected expenses, job insecurity, or investment market fluctuations?

- **Step 2: Develop Stress-Reduction Techniques:**

    o Practice stress-reduction techniques like mindfulness meditation, deep breathing exercises, or physical activity to calm your mind and regain focus.

- **Step 3: Create a Decision-Making Framework:**

- o   Establish a structured decision-making process that includes assessing your financial goals, risks, and potential outcomes before making major financial decisions.
- **Step 4: Seek Professional Guidance:**

  - o   Consider consulting a financial advisor or therapist with expertise in financial therapy to guide you through stressful financial decisions.

Tools for Stress Reduction

Explore various tools and techniques to manage stress effectively:

- **Mindfulness Meditation:** Apps like Headspace and Calm offer guided mindfulness meditation sessions to reduce stress and improve decision-making.

- **Journaling:** Keeping a financial journal to record your thoughts and emotions about money can help you gain clarity and reduce stress.

- **Financial Planning Software:** Tools like Mint and YNAB can help automate budgeting and financial planning, reducing the mental burden of tracking expenses.

Case Study: John's Stress Management Journey

John faced significant stress related to his job and mounting debts. He began practicing mindfulness meditation and adopted a structured decision-making process. Over time, his stress levels decreased, and he made more confident and rational financial choices, ultimately improving his financial well-being.

Checklist: Managing Stress in Financial Decision-Making

Before making significant financial decisions, consider these steps:

- Have you identified the stressors influencing your financial choices?
- Are you practicing stress-reduction techniques regularly?
- Have you established a structured decision-making process for important financial matters?

In the next chapters, we'll explore further strategies to enhance your financial and mental well-being while navigating the intricate relationship between money and stress. Remember that managing stress is not just about making better financial decisions; it's about improving your overall quality of life.

Chapter 5: Building Financial Resilience

In a world where financial ups and downs are inevitable, building financial resilience becomes paramount for maintaining both financial and mental well-being. In this chapter, we'll explore the concept of financial resilience, understanding what it means and how you can cultivate it to thrive in the face of adversity.

The Concept of Financial Resilience

Financial resilience refers to your ability to weather financial challenges and setbacks without experiencing severe negative impacts on your well-being. It's about bouncing back from financial hardships and maintaining financial stability even when faced with adversity.

- **Why Financial Resilience Matters:** Financial resilience is crucial because life is unpredictable. Unexpected expenses, job losses, and economic downturns can happen to anyone at any time. Having financial resilience means you're better equipped to handle these challenges without succumbing to overwhelming stress.

Practical Steps for Enhancing Financial Resilience

Building financial resilience is a deliberate and ongoing process. Here are practical steps to help you enhance your financial resilience:

- **Step 1: Emergency Fund Creation:**

    o Establish an emergency fund that covers three to six months' worth of living expenses. This financial cushion can help you stay afloat during unexpected setbacks without resorting to debt.

- **Step 2: Debt Management:**

  o Prioritize debt reduction to lower your financial obligations. Reducing debt decreases your financial vulnerability during tough times.

- **Step 3: Diversify Income Sources:**

  o Explore alternative income streams, such as part-time work, freelance gigs, or passive income investments. Multiple income sources provide a safety net if your primary source is compromised.

- **Step 4: Insurance Coverage:**

  o Ensure you have adequate insurance coverage, including health, disability, and life insurance. Insurance can protect you and your loved ones from financial catastrophe in case of illness or unexpected events.

- **Step 5: Continuous Learning:**

  o Invest in financial education and stay updated on personal finance topics. Being financially informed equips you with the knowledge to make sound decisions even during challenging times.

Coping Strategies for Financial Setbacks

Despite your best efforts, financial setbacks may occur. Here are coping strategies to navigate them:

- **Acceptance and Adaptation:** Recognize that financial setbacks are a part of life. Adapt to the situation and create a revised financial plan.

- **Seek Professional Advice:** Consult with financial advisors or therapists specializing in financial therapy to help you cope with stress and make informed decisions.

- **Leverage Support Networks:** Lean on friends and family for emotional support and potential financial assistance if needed.

Case Study: Maria's Financial Resilience Journey

Maria experienced a job loss during an economic downturn. Thanks to her emergency fund and diverse income sources from freelance work, she was financially resilient and could weather the setback without experiencing severe stress or taking on excessive debt.

Checklist: Assessing Your Financial Resilience

Evaluate your current level of financial resilience with these questions:

- Do you have an emergency fund in place?
- Are you actively working to reduce debt?
- Have you diversified your income sources?
- Do you have adequate insurance coverage for various life events?

- Are you continuously learning about personal finance?

In the upcoming chapters, we'll explore strategies for nurturing your financial and mental well-being further, ensuring you're well-prepared to face any financial challenges that may come your way. Remember, financial resilience is your armor against life's uncertainties.

Chapter 6: Seeking Help: Mental Health and Financial Professionals

Navigating the complex terrain where mental health and finances intersect can be challenging. In this chapter, we'll explore the pivotal role that mental health professionals, financial advisors, and therapists specializing in financial therapy can play in helping you achieve both mental well-being and financial stability.

The Role of Mental Health Professionals

Mental health professionals, including therapists, counselors, and psychiatrists, are trained to address and support individuals dealing with various mental health concerns. When it comes to money and mental health, they can provide invaluable assistance in several ways:

- **Diagnosis and Treatment:** Mental health professionals can diagnose and treat mental health conditions like anxiety and depression that may be linked to financial stress.

- **Coping Strategies:** They can teach coping strategies and provide a safe space to explore your emotions and concerns related to money.

- **Behavioral Change:** Mental health professionals help you identify and change harmful behavioral patterns and beliefs related to money.

- **Family Dynamics:** They can address how family dynamics and relationships impact your financial and mental well-being.

The Role of Financial Advisors and Planners

Financial advisors and planners aren't just about numbers; they play a more comprehensive role in your financial well-being:

- **Financial Planning:** They help you create and execute a financial plan that aligns with your life goals and values.

- **Risk Management:** Financial professionals assess your risk tolerance and develop strategies to protect your financial assets.

- **Budgeting and Saving:** They provide guidance on budgeting, saving, and investing to build financial security.

- **Retirement Planning:** Financial advisors assist in planning for retirement, ensuring you're financially prepared for your post-work years.

Collaborative Approaches to Mental Health and Financial Wellness

In many cases, the most effective approach involves collaboration between mental health professionals and financial advisors. Here's how it works:

- **Communication:** Mental health professionals and financial advisors should communicate and coordinate their efforts to address your holistic well-being.

- **Holistic Assessment:** A comprehensive assessment of your financial and mental health is conducted, taking into account your specific circumstances and challenges.

- **Treatment Plans:** Based on the assessment, a tailored treatment plan is developed, incorporating strategies for both financial and mental well-being.

Case Study: Emma's Collaborative Journey

Emma experienced overwhelming financial stress that manifested as anxiety and depression. She sought help from a therapist specializing in financial therapy and collaborated with a financial advisor. Together, they created a plan to reduce her debt, manage her emotions around money, and set her on a path to financial and mental recovery.

Checklist: Seeking Help for Your Financial and Mental Health

Before seeking help, consider these steps:

- Assess your current financial and mental health needs.
- Research and select qualified mental health professionals and financial advisors who align with your goals.
- Prepare a list of questions and concerns to discuss with them during initial consultations.

In the chapters ahead, we'll delve deeper into strategies for nurturing your mental and financial well-being, offering insights into managing major life transitions and advocating for mental health awareness and support. Remember, seeking help is a sign of strength, and it's a vital step toward achieving both financial stability and mental wellness.

Chapter 7: Major Life Transitions and Your Financial Health

Life is a series of transitions, and how we manage these changes can significantly impact our mental and financial well-being. In this chapter, we'll explore major life transitions, such as marriage, parenthood, career changes, and retirement, and how they intersect with your financial health and mental stability. Understanding how to navigate these transitions is essential for maintaining balance and resilience.

Marriage: Combining Finances and Emotions

Marriage is a significant life transition that involves merging two lives, including finances and emotions.

- **Joint Finances:** Couples often combine their finances, creating a shared financial future. Open communication about financial goals and values is essential.

- **Financial Roles:** Determine how financial responsibilities will be divided. Will one person manage the finances, or will you share the responsibilities equally?

- **Financial Goals:** Align your financial goals and create a joint financial plan that supports your shared dreams and aspirations.

Parenthood: Financial Planning for the Future

Becoming a parent brings joy and new financial responsibilities.

- **Budget Adjustments:** Reevaluate your budget to accommodate the costs of raising a child, including childcare, education, and healthcare.

- **Insurance:** Ensure you have adequate life and health insurance coverage to protect your growing family.

- **College Savings:** Consider starting a college savings fund to prepare for your child's education expenses.

Career Changes: Navigating Job Transitions

Career changes, whether voluntary or involuntary, can impact your financial stability and mental health.

- **Emergency Fund:** Maintain a robust emergency fund to cover expenses during job transitions.

- **Skill Development:** Invest in developing new skills or certifications to enhance your employability.

- **Networking:** Build a professional network that can provide support and job opportunities during career changes.

Retirement: Transitioning to a New Phase of Life

Retirement is a significant life transition that requires careful financial planning.

- **Savings and Investments:** Ensure you have a well-funded retirement savings plan and consider how you'll invest your retirement funds to provide financial security.

- **Healthcare:** Plan for healthcare costs in retirement, including Medicare and supplemental insurance.

- **Lifestyle Adjustments:** Prepare for the emotional and lifestyle adjustments that come with retirement by defining your retirement goals and activities.

Case Study: David and Sarah's Retirement Transition

David and Sarah, a retired couple, struggled with the emotional and financial adjustment to retirement. They sought help from a financial advisor and a therapist specializing in retirement transitions. With their guidance, David and Sarah redefined their retirement goals, adjusted their financial plan, and found fulfillment in their new phase of life.

Checklist: Navigating Life Transitions Successfully

As you approach or go through major life transitions, follow these steps:

- Communicate openly with your partner about financial goals and responsibilities.
- Adjust your budget and financial plan to accommodate new expenses.

- Seek professional advice from financial planners or therapists when facing significant life changes.
- Continually evaluate and adapt your financial and mental health strategies to align with your evolving circumstances.

In the chapters ahead, we'll explore advocacy for mental health awareness, the importance of self-care, and strategies for long-term financial and mental well-being. Remember, life is full of changes, and by embracing them with a proactive mindset, you can thrive both mentally and financially.

Chapter 8: Advocating for Mental Health Awareness and Support

Advocacy for mental health awareness is crucial in breaking down stigmas and ensuring that individuals have access to the support they need. In this chapter, we'll explore the importance of advocating for mental health, both on a personal level and within your community. By becoming a mental health advocate, you can help create a more supportive and understanding environment for yourself and others.

Understanding the Importance of Mental Health Advocacy

Mental health advocacy involves speaking up for mental health rights, promoting awareness, and working to eliminate the stigma surrounding mental health conditions. Here's why it matters:

- **Stigma Reduction:** Advocacy helps reduce the stigma associated with mental health issues, making it easier for individuals to seek help without fear of judgment.

- **Access to Care:** Advocacy efforts can lead to improved access to mental health care services, ensuring that individuals in need can receive appropriate treatment and support.

- **Policy Change:** Advocacy can influence policy changes at the local, state, and national levels, leading to better mental health care and support systems.

Personal Advocacy for Mental Health

You can be a mental health advocate in your own life and community by taking these steps:

- **Step 1: Educate Yourself:** Understand mental health conditions, treatment options, and the impact of stigma. Knowledge is a powerful tool in advocacy.

- **Step 2: Share Your Story:** If you've faced mental health challenges, consider sharing your experiences to reduce stigma and provide hope to others.

- **Step 3: Support Others:** Be a listening ear and source of support for friends or family members who may be dealing with mental health issues.

- **Step 4: Advocate for Resources:** Encourage your workplace, school, or community organizations to provide mental health resources and support programs.

Community-Level Advocacy

Advocating for mental health awareness at the community level can have a significant impact:

- **Join Organizations:** Consider joining mental health advocacy organizations or local support groups to connect with like-minded individuals.

- **Raise Funds:** Participate in fundraising events or campaigns to support mental health programs and services in your community.

- **Advocate for Policy Changes:** Collaborate with local representatives and organizations to advocate for improved mental health policies and services.

Case Study: Emily's Journey as a Mental Health Advocate

Emily, who battled depression in her youth, became a mental health advocate in her community. She started a mental health support group, organized awareness events, and lobbied for improved mental health resources in local schools. Her efforts not only helped others but also contributed to a more inclusive and understanding community.

Checklist: Becoming a Mental Health Advocate

To become a mental health advocate, consider these steps:

- Educate yourself about mental health and stigma.
- Share your experiences or support others in sharing their stories.
- Participate in mental health-related events or organizations.
- Advocate for mental health resources and support in your community.

In the final chapters, we'll explore the importance of self-care and strategies for long-term financial and mental well-being. Remember that by advocating for mental health, you can make a positive impact on your own life and the lives of those around you.

Chapter 9: The Power of Self-Care

Self-care is a vital component of maintaining good mental health, and it plays a significant role in our financial well-being as well. In this chapter, we'll explore how self-care practices can boost your mental resilience and help you make sound financial decisions, ultimately leading to a healthier, more balanced life.

The Interconnection of Self-Care and Financial Health

Self-care is not just about bubble baths and spa days; it's a holistic approach to maintaining mental and emotional well-being. When you practice self-care, you're better equipped to manage stress, make thoughtful financial choices, and nurture your financial health.

Self-Care for Mental Health

Here are some self-care practices that can benefit your mental health:

- **Mindfulness Meditation:** Regular meditation can reduce stress and anxiety, helping you stay calm and focused when making financial decisions.

- **Exercise:** Physical activity releases endorphins, which boost mood and reduce stress. Exercise can also be an inexpensive form of self-care.

- **Healthy Eating:** A balanced diet provides essential nutrients that support brain function and emotional stability. Avoiding excessive sugar and caffeine can also help regulate mood.

- **Quality Sleep:** Adequate sleep is crucial for mental health and cognitive function. Poor sleep can lead to impulsive financial decisions.

Self-Care for Financial Health

Practicing self-care can also improve your financial well-being:

- **Budgeting:** Regularly reviewing your budget and financial goals is a form of self-care. It helps you stay in control and make adjustments as needed.

- **Debt Management:** Taking steps to reduce debt is a form of financial self-care. It lowers financial stress and improves your overall financial picture.

- **Emergency Fund:** Building and maintaining an emergency fund is a financial safety net that provides peace of mind during unexpected events.

- **Financial Education:** Continuously learning about personal finance is a valuable form of self-care. It empowers you to make informed financial decisions.

Case Study: Ryan's Self-Care Journey

Ryan struggled with anxiety related to his job and finances. He adopted self-care practices like regular exercise and mindfulness meditation. Over time, he found that his mental resilience improved, allowing him to make more confident and rational financial choices.

Checklist: Incorporating Self-Care into Your Routine

To integrate self-care into your daily life, consider these steps:

- Identify self-care practices that resonate with you and fit your lifestyle.
- Create a self-care routine that includes both mental and financial well-being activities.
- Prioritize self-care and make it a non-negotiable part of your daily or weekly schedule.

In the final chapter, we'll summarize key takeaways and provide a roadmap for long-term financial and mental well-being. Remember that self-care is an essential ingredient in the recipe for a healthier, more fulfilling life.

Chapter 10: Navigating Your Financial and Mental Well-Being Journey

Congratulations! You've embarked on a journey to understand the intricate link between your financial and mental health. In this final chapter, we'll recap key takeaways, provide a roadmap for your long-term well-being, and offer a vision of a balanced and fulfilled life where your financial health supports your mental wellness.

Recap of Key Takeaways

Let's review the essential insights from this book:

1. **The Connection:** Your financial and mental health are intricately linked. Financial stress can harm your mental well-being, and poor mental health can lead to financial difficulties.

2. **Budgeting:** Creating and sticking to a budget is a foundational step for both financial and mental health. It provides clarity, reduces anxiety, and empowers better financial decisions.

3. **Savings and Emergency Funds:** Building an emergency fund is a form of financial self-care. It provides security and peace of mind in times of uncertainty.

4. **Debt Management:** Reducing and managing debt lowers financial stress and supports mental wellness.

5. **Stress and Decision-Making:** Stress can lead to impulsive financial decisions. Managing stress is crucial for making sound financial choices.

6. **Financial Resilience:** Building financial resilience through savings, diversified income sources, and insurance protects your financial and mental well-being.

7. **Seeking Help:** Mental health professionals, financial advisors, and therapists specializing in financial therapy can provide valuable support during challenging times.

8. **Life Transitions:** Major life transitions, such as marriage, parenthood, career changes, and retirement, require careful financial planning and emotional resilience.

9. **Advocacy:** Advocating for mental health awareness and support creates a more inclusive and understanding community.

10. **Self-Care:** Self-care practices improve both mental and financial health by reducing stress and promoting well-being.

Your Roadmap to Long-Term Well-Being

Here's your roadmap for long-term financial and mental well-being:

1. **Self-Assessment:** Continuously evaluate your financial and mental health. Recognize when you need support and seek help when necessary.

2. **Budget and Emergency Fund:** Maintain a budget and an emergency fund to provide financial stability.

3. **Debt Management:** Prioritize debt reduction to lower financial stress.

4. **Stress Management:** Develop stress-reduction techniques and a structured decision-making process for financial choices.

5. **Financial Resilience:** Diversify income sources, invest in insurance, and continuously educate yourself about personal finance.

6. **Seeking Help:** Don't hesitate to consult professionals when dealing with mental health or complex financial issues.

7. **Life Transitions:** Plan for major life transitions, adjusting your financial and emotional strategies accordingly.

8. **Advocacy:** Advocate for mental health awareness and support in your community.

9. **Self-Care:** Incorporate self-care practices into your daily routine to nurture both your mental and financial health.

A Vision for a Balanced Life

In the ideal balance between financial and mental well-being, you'll find:

* Financial stability that supports your life goals and aspirations.
* Emotional resilience to navigate life's challenges.
* The ability to make thoughtful financial choices that align with your values and priorities.
* A supportive community that understands the importance of mental health.

Conclusion

Your journey to understanding the connection between money and mental health is ongoing. By applying the principles and strategies from this book, you're on your way to achieving a life where your financial and mental well-being coexist harmoniously, bringing you fulfillment, peace, and happiness.

Thank you for joining us on this journey, and remember that your financial and mental health are worth every effort you invest in them.

Chapter 11: Embracing Financial and Mental Well-Being for the Long Term

You've reached the final chapter of your journey toward understanding the profound connection between financial and mental health. In this chapter, we'll explore how to integrate the principles you've learned into your daily life, ensuring lasting well-being for years to come.

Creating a Sustainable Financial and Mental Well-Being Lifestyle

Achieving financial and mental well-being is not a one-time endeavor; it's an ongoing commitment. Here's how you can create a sustainable lifestyle that nurtures both aspects of your health:

Step 1: Set Clear Goals

Define your financial and mental health goals. What do you want to achieve in both areas? Having clear objectives will provide direction and motivation.

Step 2: Create a Holistic Plan

Develop a comprehensive plan that encompasses both financial and mental health strategies. Ensure they complement each other and align with your goals.

Step 3: Prioritize Self-Care

Make self-care a non-negotiable part of your routine. Whether it's daily meditation, weekly exercise, or monthly financial check-ins, prioritize activities that promote well-being.

Step 4: Embrace Financial Resilience

Continue to build financial resilience by maintaining your emergency fund, diversifying income sources, and staying informed about personal finance.

Step 5: Seek Professional Support

Regularly consult with mental health professionals and financial advisors. They can provide guidance, monitor progress, and help you adapt your strategies as needed.

Step 6: Cultivate a Supportive Community

Surround yourself with a supportive network of friends and family who understand the importance of both financial and mental health. Share your journey with them.

Step 7: Continuously Learn and Grow

Stay curious and open to learning. The worlds of finance and mental health are constantly evolving. Stay informed about new strategies and techniques.

Sustaining Balance: Real-Life Examples

Here are two examples of individuals who have successfully integrated financial and mental well-being into their lives:

1. **Sarah's Journey:** Sarah, a single mother, faced financial stress while managing her job and family. She incorporated stress-reduction techniques into her daily routine, sought financial advice, and gradually reduced her debt. Over time, she achieved

a harmonious balance between her financial and mental health, providing a secure and nurturing environment for her family.

2. **Mark's Financial Resilience:** Mark, a young professional, consistently saved a portion of his income, diversified his investments, and secured insurance coverage. When he faced an unexpected job loss, he had the financial resilience to navigate the challenge without succumbing to stress. His mental well-being remained stable, allowing him to secure a new job with confidence.

Checklist for Long-Term Well-Being

Use this checklist to maintain your financial and mental well-being over the long term:

*   Set clear goals for both financial and mental health.
*   Create a holistic plan that integrates both aspects of your well-being.
*   Prioritize self-care practices that nurture your mental and financial health.
*   Continuously build financial resilience through savings and diversification.
*   Regularly seek guidance from professionals.
*   Cultivate a supportive community.
*   Stay committed to lifelong learning.

Conclusion: Your Ongoing Journey

Your journey to understanding the profound connection between money and mental health doesn't end here. It's a lifelong path of growth, learning, and self-discovery. By applying the principles and strategies you've acquired, you're equipped to lead a fulfilling life where financial and mental well-being coexist harmoniously. Embrace this journey with enthusiasm, knowing that your well-being is worth every effort you invest in it.

Appendix: Additional Resources and Tools for Financial and Mental Well-Being

In this appendix, you'll find a wealth of additional resources, tools, and information to support your journey toward understanding and improving the link between your financial and mental health. These resources include websites, books, apps, and organizations that can provide further guidance and assistance.

Websites and Online Communities

1. **National Alliance on Mental Illness (NAMI):** Visit NAMI for a wide range of resources on mental health awareness, support, and advocacy.

2. **Financial Planning Association (FPA):** The FPA offers articles, tools, and directories to help you find a certified financial planner near you.

3. **Mental Health America:** Check out Mental Health America for information on various mental health topics, screenings, and resources.

4. **Investopedia:** This financial education platform, Investopedia, offers articles, tutorials, and tools to enhance your financial literacy.

5. **Personal Finance Subreddit:** Join the Personal Finance subreddit to engage in discussions, seek advice, and learn from others' experiences.

Books for Financial Literacy and Mental Health

1. **"Your Money or Your Life" by Vicki Robin and Joe Dominguez:** This classic book helps you transform your relationship with money and achieve financial independence.

2. **"The Total Money Makeover" by Dave Ramsey:** Dave Ramsey provides a step-by-step plan for getting out of debt, building an emergency fund, and securing your financial future.

3. **"The Happiness Advantage" by Shawn Achor:** Discover how positive psychology can boost your mental well-being and success in this insightful book.

4. **"Mind Over Money" by Brad Klontz and Ted Klontz:** Learn about the psychological barriers to financial success and how to overcome them.

Mobile Apps for Financial Management and Mental Wellness

1. **Mint:** This popular app helps you track and manage your finances, create budgets, and set financial goals.

2. **Calm:** Use the Calm app for guided meditation, mindfulness exercises, and stress reduction techniques.

3. **You Need a Budget (YNAB):** YNAB is a budgeting app that focuses on giving every dollar a job and helping you gain control of your finances.

4. **Headspace:** Headspace offers guided meditation sessions and sleep stories to improve your mental well-being.

Financial Education and Mental Health Organizations

1. **Financial Therapy Association (FTA):** The FTA provides resources and information on the intersection of finance and therapy.

2. **American Psychological Association (APA):** The APA offers articles, publications, and resources on mental health.

3. **National Endowment for Financial Education (NEFE):** NEFE provides resources and tools to promote financial literacy and well-being.

4. **Anxiety and Depression Association of America (ADAA):** The ADAA offers resources and support for those dealing with anxiety and depression.

Checklists for Ongoing Well-Being

1. **Financial Checkup Checklist:**

   - Review your budget and adjust it as needed.
   - Ensure your emergency fund is adequately funded.
   - Evaluate your investments and retirement savings.
   - Check your credit report for inaccuracies.
   - Review your insurance coverage and update it if necessary.

2. **Mental Health Maintenance Checklist:**

- Prioritize self-care activities in your daily routine.
- Maintain regular check-ins with your mental health professional.
- Stay connected with a support network of friends and family.
- Engage in stress-reduction techniques like meditation or exercise.
- Continue learning about mental health through books, articles, or courses.

Conclusion

Your journey to understanding the profound connection between your financial and mental health is a continuous and enriching experience. These additional resources and tools are here to support you in your ongoing efforts to achieve lasting well-being. Remember that investing in your financial and mental health is an investment in your future happiness and success.

www.ingramcontent.com/pod-product-compliance
Lightning Source LLC
Chambersburg PA
CBHW062303290526
45794CB00006B/2678